YOUR GUIDE TO
PLANNING THE
WEDDING DAY

Carole Chapman

foulsham
LONDON • NEW YORK • TORONTO • SYDNEY

foulsham
Bennetts Close, Cippenham, Berks. SL1 5AP

Disclaimer
While every effort has been made to ensure the
accuracy of all the information contained within
this book, neither the author nor the publisher
can be liable for any errors. In particular, since
laws change from time to time, it is vital that
each individual checks relevant legal details for
themselves.

ISBN 0-572-01874-6

Phototypeset in Great Britain by Typesetting Solutions, Slough, Berks.
Printed and bound in Great Britain by Cox & Wyman Ltd., Reading, Berks.

YOUR GUIDE TO
PLANNING THE WEDDING DAY

Other titles in The Wedding Collection:

Contents

Introduction

◆ ◆ ◆

This book is a handy guide to getting married. Its aim is to take some of the hard work out of the planning stages, and it is full of useful tips and lists which can be used to plan the wedding and check off the arrangements and preparations as they are made.

It is a practical book, and does not pretend to offer anything other than practical advice. The material has been drawn from a number of authoritative sources and is presented helpfully and concisely.

The book is intended for couples planning their wedding and for those involved in helping with the organising, such as the bride's parents, the best man and chief bridesmaid.

Preparing for Life Together

Every bride and groom spares some thought to what married life will hold and how they will get on living with each other.

Living with Each Other

It is vital that time is spent learning to communicate about both important and everyday issues. A good marriage does not merely evolve, it demands a great deal of commitment. With love and the desire to be together, all the effort is worthwhile.

Accommodation

Buying a Home
It may seem attractive to purchase a house but of course this is an expensive commitment. Mortgages can be obtained from building societies, banks and other organisations. It is vital to take good advice about the amount of money that you can realistically borrow for a mortgage as this will, most likely, be the largest loan that any couple takes on.

Renting a Home
Rented accommodation provides independence without the financial strains involved in taking out a mortgage. It can provide the opportunity to save enough capital for a substantial deposit on a subsequent house purchase, thereby reducing mortgage payments for the future.

Sharing a Home
Financial responsibilities and chores may be shared and companionship can be welcome, but good communication is essential for any such arrangement to work. Practicalities must be considered realistically!

Joint Finances

When married, it may be advisable to arrange joint finances for convenience of management. Some couples have a joint bank account for household expenses, while keeping their personal spending money separate.

Pensions

Retirement may seem a long way off, but it is important to provide for it as early as possible. If there is no company pension scheme, it is prudent to take out an affordable plan.

Insurance

Life
It is advisable to arrange life insurance in each other's favour.

Buildings
House buildings insurance is obligatory when buying a house.

House Contents
House contents should be insured against possible loss from theft and fire. The policy should cover the replacement value as new and be upgraded every year to keep pace with inflation.

Finances

Day-to-day finances must be organised carefully. A simple, but honest, budget will provide the guidelines necessary to assess realistic spending power.

Checklist 1 FINANCE

	£ pa	£ pm	£ pw
Income (net)			
Husband			
Wife			
Other			
Total			
Outgoings			
House			
Mortgage/rent			
Insurance			
Loans			
Water rates			
Gas			
Electricity			
Telephone			
TV			
Repairs/decorations			
Food/cleaning			
Council Tax			
Travelling			
Clothes, etc.			
Medical			
Leisure			
Savings			
Pensions			
Other			
TOTALS			

Engagement

◆

Announcements

It is important to ensure that there are no objections to the marriage. Both sets of parents should be informed as soon as possible and it is traditional for the bride's parents to be the first to learn the news. If the two sets of parents are unacquainted, arrangements should be made for them to meet each other.

Informal

Close relatives and friends may be informed personally, by letter or by telephone. The following list may be used to ensure that family and friends have been informed.

Checklist 2 INFORMAL ANNOUNCEMENTS																			
Done ✔																			
Tel. No.																			
Tel. call ✔																			
Done ✔																			
Address																			
Letter ✔																			
Visit ✔																			
Name																			

Formal

The bride or the bride's mother usually sends an announcement to the local press stating the details, for example:

> **Mr S South and**
> **Miss/Ms N North**
> The engagement is announced between
> Sam, only son of Mr and Mrs Sid South of Southton and
> Nel, eldest daughter of Mr and Mrs Ned North of Northton

When to Marry

Marriages may take place between 0800 and 1800 on any day except Christmas Day. They are not generally allowed in churches on Sundays.

Checklist 3 **SETTING THE DATE**

Wedding

Day _____

Date _____

Time _____

Availability of

Best man

Chief bridesmaid

Bridesmaid

Bridesmaid

Flower girl

Page boy

Page boy

Page boy

Chief usher

Usher

Usher

Parents: Bride's

　　　　Groom's

Church/Register Office

Honeymoon

Dates　　　　From _____ To _____

Notes　　　　_____

_____

_____

_____

Type of Wedding

Church or Register Office
The choice between a church or civil ceremony largely depends on religious beliefs.

Double
Double weddings can be very special occasions and usually take place when two siblings decide to marry at the same time. They do save time and administration, but the arrangements for processions and order of speeches at the reception need careful planning.

Breaking the Engagement

Breaking the engagement can be painful but it is much less painful than a broken marriage! Relations and friends can be informed quietly. If the engagement is broken by the bride-to-be, she should return the engagement ring, but if the groom-to-be is responsible, his betrothed is entitled to keep the ring.

Legal Requirements

◆

Ministers and local registrars should be consulted about the legal requirements as they are able to explain the simplest and best methods for each individual. To summarise a few points, here are some brief guidelines.

Who can Conduct the Ceremony?

In England and Wales, a marriage must be solemnized by an authorised person, such as:
— the registrar of any register office;
— ordained ministers of the Church of England;
— ministers of other religious denominations who have been legally authorised to register marriages.

Sex

In the UK, one partner must have been born male and the other female.

Minimum Age

Both partners must be over the age of 16. If either is under 18 and unmarried, the parent's or guardian's legal consent is necessary. However, someone between the ages of 16 and 18 who has been divorced or widowed does not need parental consent.

Witnesses

The parties to the marriage must arrange for the attendance of two witnesses to be present at the marriage and to sign the register.

Timing

The hours between which weddings may take place are 0800 and 1800, unless it is to be a Jewish or Quaker wedding.

Relations who may not Marry

Marriages between close family and blood relatives are not permitted; a marriage solemnized between persons within the following degrees of relationship is void:

For Men	For Women
Mother	Father
Adoptive mother or former adoptive mother	Adoptive father or former adoptive father
Daughter	Son
Adoptive daughter or former adoptive daughter	Adoptive son or former adoptive son
Father's mother	Father's father
Mother's mother	Mother's father
Son's daughter	Son's son
Daughter's daughter	Daughter's son
Sister	Brother
Father's sister	Father's brother
Mother's sister	Mother's brother
Brother's daughter	Brother's son
Sister's daughter	Sister's son

Note: A "brother" and "sister" include a brother or sister of the half-blood.

Prohibited Marriages

Marriage is prohibited between persons within certain degrees of affinity, unless certain conditions are met:

For Men	For Women
Daughter of former wife	Son of former husband
Former wife of father	Former husband of mother
Former wife of father's father	Former husband of father's mother
Former wife of mother's father	Former husband of mother's mother
Daughter of son of former wife	Son of son of former husband
Daughter of daughter of former wife	Son of daughter of former husband

The conditions under which a marriage within the above degrees of affinity are permissible must be checked with the minister or Superintendent Registrar.

Second Marriages

No person who is already married to a living spouse may marry someone else. If they do so, the second marriage is invalid.

No person who is going through a divorce may marry until the decree absolute has been granted.

There is no limit to the number of times a person may marry as long as they are free to do so, but some ministers may refuse to conduct the ceremony for second and subsequent marriages.

The law of England and Wales recognizes a divorced person as 'single' so long as they can produce a decree absolute, after which a remarriage in a register office is conducted in exactly the same way as a first marriage. A decree nisi pronounces the divorce, but neither party is free to remarry until a decree absolute has been granted and obtained. This is obtainable on application by the successful petitioner six weeks after the decree nisi.

In Scotland a preliminary pronouncement does not exist; the decree is absolute (or final) from the time of the divorce, leaving the divorced person free to take steps towards remarriage if they should so desire.

British Subjects Marrying Abroad

The law is not the same for British subjects marrying abroad. The couple should consult a member of the British Embassy, Legation or Consulate in the country and district where the marriage is to take place.

British Subjects Marrying Foreigners

Whether at home or abroad, there is always the matter of nationality after marriage. The couple should seek the advice of the appropriate authorities.

Foreigners Marrying in the United Kingdom

The law is not the same for foreigners marrying in the United Kingdom. The couple should seek an interview with the clergyman or leader of the appropriate religious sect or consult a superintendent registrar's office. They should also consult their resident representative in Britain to ensure that the marriage will be legally binding in their own country.

The Merits of Marriage

Marriage gives protection in the event of separation, divorce or the death of one partner, whereas for unmarried couples, there is no clearly defined legislation.

Property
An unmarried couple need to consult a solicitor so that a written agreement can be drawn up that will cater for separation. They should also make legally valid and up-to-date wills in favour of each other.

Children
If a married couple separates or divorces, the law attempts to deal with custody/access to children. For separated unmarried couples, there is no legislation. Couples with dependant children are certainly very well advised to consider marriage.

Civil Ceremony

The Register Office

The Ceremony
A civil ceremony at a register office is a shorter and much less formal affair than a church wedding. It entails no religious service, but vows are exchanged and the register is signed by each of the newly-weds and the two witnesses. A register office cannot accommodate too many people so the guests are likely to be limited to the couple's immediate family and closest friends.

The ceremony takes approximately ten minutes and the wedding party needs to arrive at the correct time so that other bookings remain unaffected.

Preparations
The superintendent registrar should be consulted as soon as possible as it is important to ascertain the legal formalities of residence qualification and obtain a licence.

There are no bridesmaids or page boys.

Attire
A bride will often wear a special dress or early cocktail attire, carry a small bouquet and wear a hat instead of a veil. Grooms often wear dark suits.

Second Marriages

Second marriages generally have more informal and quieter celebrations than first marriages, especially if both partners are divorced. The ceremony is likely to be a civil one if either of the partners is divorced.

Checklist 4 **CIVIL CEREMONY**		
Register office		
Address		
Tel		
Superintendent registrar		
Ceremony		
Date		
Time		
No. of guests		
	Notes	£
Certificate/licence		
Music		
Flowers		
Photographs		
Video		
Confetti		
Other		
TOTAL	£	

Church Wedding

The Church

It is customary for weddings to take place in the bride's parish church. The tradition of banns invites the public to declare whether they know of any just cause or impediment against the marriage.

To marry in a different church, the minister of that church must be consulted and whatever the circumstances, the minister should be approached as soon as possible so that he may advise accordingly. Waiting lists are common at certain times of the year.

Marriage Preparation Sessions

The minister will see the couple nearer the wedding date to explain the vows and may recommend attendance at preparation sessions to discuss in detail the significance and commitment of marriage.

Giving Away

The person who gives the bride away is usually her father, but can be anyone else, or the 'giving-away ceremony' may be omitted from the service altogether.

Service

There may be a choice of service. The Book of Common Prayer of 1662 involves the bride promising to obey her husband, whereas the later version of 1928 excludes reference to obedience. The Alternative Service of 1980 leaves obedience to the couple and offers a selection of prayers.

Order
The couple need to establish the exact order in which the elements of the service will occur.

Vows
There is the option to repeat short phrases after the minister or learn phrases by rote.

Music

The choice of music helps to create the desired atmosphere and should be suitable for playing on the church organ. Music needs to be chosen before a decision is made concerning the wording for the order of service sheets.

Confetti

Confetti can make a mess of the churchyard and is often not allowed for this reason. Local litter laws must be observed! Rice, grain, fresh flower/rose petals or wild bird food are more acceptable alternative forms of confetti.

Photographs and Videos

Photographs and videos may be allowed in church if flash is not used. The minister's instructions must be followed.

Rehearsal

There is usually a rehearsal a week or so before the event so that the wedding party members are clear about the procedures for the day.

Fees

It is advisable to pay fees in advance so that there is less to deal with on the day itself.

Checklist 5 CHURCH ORDER OF SERVICE	

Before
  Music
  Bells	

Arrival of bride Music	
Entry of bride Music	
Minister's intro Hymn	
Ceremony Hymn	
Prayers	
Signing of register Music	
Leaving church Music	
Bells	

Checklist 6   CHURCH ARRANGEMENTS

	£
Church	
Name	
Address	
Tel	
Minister	
Verger	
Organist	
Choir	
Bells	
Ceremony	
Date	
Time	
Banns dates	1
	2
	3
Licence/certificate	
obtained ☐	
Flowers	
Photos/video	
Confetti	
Preparation sessions	1
Dates and times	2
	3
Rehearsal date and	
time	
Fees - payment time	
Other fees	
TOTAL £	

Finance

Responsibility for Payment

Traditionally the major burden has fallen on the bride's father but since a wedding can be very expensive today, both families tend to share the financial responsibility. If the couple are older than the traditional age for first marriages, it may be inappropriate for parents to be expected to pay, in which case the couple should take over all of the expenses.

If the two sets of parents are contributing, they should be encouraged to negotiate at an early stage.

Financial Arrangements

Agreements
It is wise to obtain written agreements for supplies and services.

Contracts
Contracts for goods and services should be read carefully and fully understood.

Estimates and Quotations
Estimates provide only a general idea of final cost whereas quotations usually state fixed prices for specified jobs. For this reason quotations are preferable. Detailed information about quotations and suppliers of goods and services is given at the end of this chapter.

Deposits
It is reasonable for a supplier to demand a deposit, but it is important to check the procedure in the event of cancellation.

Budget

Regardless of who is paying, a detailed budget should be devised to ensure that the style of wedding chosen can realistically be afforded. It may be helpful to know who traditionally pays for the various expenses, and this is indicated in the columns on the Budget List at the end of this chapter.

Priorities

When compiling a draft budget the bride will need an idea of priorities. The following list may be shuffled to create the most favoured order of priority.

Checklist 7 **PRIORITIES**		
	Priority Order	Item
Reception venue	1	
Food	2	
Cake	3	
Drink	4	
Music	5	
Wedding dress	6	
Groom's attire	7	
Photos/video	8	
Flowers	9	
Invitations	10	
	11	
	12	
	13	
	14	
	15	
	16	
	17	
	18	
	19	
	20	

Budget

Having decided priorities, estimates or quotations should be obtained. If these exceed the funds available, they will need modification until the budget falls within the decided target.

Final Budget

When the overall draft budget has been modified to suit funds available, it will be possible to finalise plans. As actual costs become evident, these may be entered on the Budget List so that it represents a full, accurate and up-to-date record of finances. 'Savings' may be transferred to other areas.

Checklist 8 **BUDGET LIST**		Estimate	Quotation
		£	£
Contingency: Allow an extra 5-10%			
ATTIRE			
Bride			
Wedding	Dress		
	Train		
	Veil/hat		
	Shoes		
	Underwear		
	Hosiery		
	Something old		
	new		
	borrowed		
	blue		
	Jewellery		
	Perfume		
Going Away	Outfit		
Bridesmaids	Dresses		
	Headdresses		
	Shoes		
	Hosiery		
Page boys	Outfits		
	Shoes		
Ushers	Outfits		
	Shoes		
Groom			
Wedding	Suit		
	Shoes		
	Shirt		
	Tie		
Going-away	Outfit		

Final (showing traditional payers)		Deposit	Balance	Paid
£ (bride)	£ (groom)	£	£	✔
✔				
✔				
✔				
✔				
✔				
✔				
✔				
✔				
✔				
✔				
✔				
✔				
✔				
✔				
✔				
✔				
✔				
✔				
✔				
✔				
	✔			
	✔			
	✔			
	✔			
	✔			

Checklist 8 BUDGET LIST (cont.)

		Estimate £	Quotation £
Contingency: Allow an extra 5-10%			
ATTIRE			
Best man	Suit		
	Shoes		
	Shirt		
	Tie		
	Umbrella		
TRANSPORT			
To ceremony	Bride		
	Bride's father		
	Bride's mother		
	Bridesmaids		
	Groom and best man		
To reception	Bride's father and mother		
	Groom and best man		
From reception	Bride and groom		
Decorations			
PHOTOGRAPHS/VIDEO			
FLOWERS	Church		
	Reception		
	Bride's bouquet		
	Bridesmaids' bouquets		
	Mothers' corsages		
	Groom's buttonhole		
	Fathers' x2 buttonholes		
	Best man's buttonhole		
	Ushers' buttonholes		

Final (showing traditional payers)		Deposit	Balance	Paid
£ (bride)	£ (groom)	£	£	✔
✔				
✔				
✔				
✔				
	✔			
✔				
	✔			
	✔			
	✔			
✔				
✔				
✔				
	✔			
	✔			
	✔			
	✔			
	✔			
	✔			
	✔			

Checklist 8 **BUDGET LIST (cont.)**

		Estimate	Quotation
		£	£
Contingency: Allow an extra 5-10%			
CHURCH/	Minister		
REGISTER	Banns		
OFFICE	Licence/Certificate		
	Verger		
	Organist		
	Choir		
	Bell ringers		
	Collection		
ACCOMMODATION	Attendants		
	Guests		
RECEPTION	Hire		
	Decorations		
	Furniture		
	Caterer		
	Servers		
	Equipment Crockery		
	Cutlery		
	Glasses		
	Insurance		
	Food Menus		
	Cake		
	Drink Meal		
	Toasts		
	Other		
	Barman		
	Entertainment		
	Service charge		
	Tips		

Final (showing traditional payers)		Deposit	Balance	Paid
£ (bride)	£ (groom)	£	£	✔
	✔			
	✔			
	✔			
	✔			
	✔			
	✔			
	✔			
	✔			
✔				
✔				
✔				
✔				
✔				
✔				
✔				
✔				
✔				
✔				
✔				
✔				
✔				
✔				
✔				
✔				
✔				
✔				

Checklist 8 **BUDGET LIST (cont.)**	Estimate	Quotation
	£	£
Contingency: Allow an extra 5-10%		
HONEYMOON Travel		
Accommodation		
Attire		
Spending money		
Documentation		
Passports/Visas		
Maps/Guide Books		
Medical inoculations		
Insurance		
PRESS Before wedding		
ANNOUNCEMENTS After wedding		
STATIONERY Invitations Cards		
Envelopes		
Maps		
Postage		
Order of service sheets		
Menus		
Place name cards		
Seating plan chart		
Cake boxes & inners		
Other		
Bridal notepaper		
Thank you Letters		
Envelopes		
Postage		.
Diary		
Keepsake album/file		
Guest book		

Final (showing traditional payers)		Deposit	Balance	Paid
£ (bride)	£ (groom)	£	£	✔
	✔			
	✔			
	✔			
	✔			
	✔			
	✔			
	✔			
	✔			
	✔			
✔				
✔				
✔				
✔				
✔				
✔				
✔				
✔				
✔				
✔				
✔				
✔				
✔				
✔				
✔				
✔				
✔				
✔				
✔				

Checklist 8 **BUDGET LIST** (cont.)		Estimate	Quotation
		£	£
Contingency: Allow an extra 5-10%			
BEAUTY			
TREATMENTS			
Bride	Hairdresser		
	Make-up		
	General		
	Fitness		
Groom	Barber		
GIFTS			
To groom	Ring		
	Gift		
To bride	**Rings** Engagement		
	Wedding		
	Gift		
To bridesmaids			
To page boys			
To best man			
To ushers			
PRE-WEDDING			
PARTIES	Rehearsal		
	Hen		
	Stag		
PETTY CASH	For best man		
SPECIAL			
SERVICES			
TOTAL			

Final (showing traditional payers)		Deposit	Balance	Paid
£ (bride)	£ (groom)	£	£	✔
✔				
✔				
✔				
✔				
	✔			
✔				
✔				
	✔			
	✔			
	✔			
	✔			
	✔			
	✔			
	✔			
✔				
✔				
	✔			
	✔			

Suppliers of Goods and Services

Contact should be made with as many suppliers as possible in the early stages of the arrangements. Quotations will be needed for everything. Yes, everything! This wedding business is expensive and the least anyone should do is make sure that money is spent with the most competitive suppliers.

The bride will probably have very little experience in negotiating prices, or obtaining competitive quotations for that matter, so careful attention paid here may save many hundreds of pounds in the weeks and months to follow.

The first thing to be done in regard to any quotation is to decide on needs. This is not as easy as it sounds because new ideas can be very tempting and they produce last-minute additions and changes. These are invariably very expensive because they are charged "outside" of the original quotation. So above all at the outset, it is important to try to ensure that all needs are included before the final quotations are obtained.

Step one is to search the Yellow Pages and note convenient or likely suppliers from its various sections; not one from each section, but several. This may be impossible for say, bridal dress shops, but in regard to caterers, photographers, Limousine drivers, reception venues, florists, etc., then six or more may be appropriate. So, onto the method for searching through the Yellow Pages.

First, the sections for consideration. They are: Wedding Services, where almost every conceivable wedding option will be advertised; Places of Worship; Ladies Wear; Halls; Caterers; Hotels and Inns; Bakers and Confectioners; Car Hire — Chauffeur Driver; Florists; Photographers — General; Toastmasters; Discos — Mobile; Balloons and Novelty; Party Planners; Men's Wear!

Bearing in mind the need for several from the nominated sections, it is suggested that the choice is made from only those contacts who have the local telephone exchange number. This ought to be the same as the telephone exchange at work to place purchaser and supplier in the same working community. The work place is generally best because it is possible to keep things moving along in the lunch hour — every day if necessary.

A telephone call to each supplier will reveal the sort of price level they envisage for the particular wedding. They should be informed that they will be given a chance to make a formal quotation, but that for the purpose of planning the budget an educated estimate of eventual costs is necesssary at this early stage. This exercise will identify the more expensive contacts and provide an idea about which of them was the most helpful.

The next step ought to be a discussion with each of these various suppliers. They will all have much more experience about what ought to go into a successful wedding than the bride. So it is not a bad idea to be led by them — at first. On the basis that the bride wants her day to be memorable, pretty and "the best", she should start at the top of her list and aim to sit down for a chat with one of the more expensive of them.

Some of these meetings will be much easier than others because the options are more readily understood. For instance, if the bride wants to be driven in a Rolls Royce, there may be nothing further to discuss, but if the White Mercedes is half the price, then at least the bride ought to know that this is the case. Another point is to make sure that the driver guarantees that there will be no pressure during the wedding, just because he is booked to drive another bride immediately afterwards!

Other meetings will be more difficult; flowers can be arranged everywhere if the bride is not careful and catering can become a maze in itself. Where necessary then, help and advice should be sought and if this is not forthcoming, other suppliers can be consulted. There is absolutely no point in any of the suppliers asking about "wants" until the bride is clear about her needs. Only then can she be sensible about what can be afforded. If contacts are unhelpful about understanding basic needs, then they should be crossed off the list and another supplier considered.

When the bride has had time to digest the advice and literature from the "top end" suppliers she should be in a much better position to make decisions. She will have an idea of likely cost, the amount she is prepared to pay and will have a better understanding of the standards she wants to maintain. Equally she will probably learn which aspects of the day are unaffordable.

This is the time to get the first quotations. A specification of requirements based on everything learned should be drawn up and sent to all contacts inviting them to quote. Each supplier should receive exactly the same specification as this is the only way that, when the replies are received, a true comparison of values on a like-with-like basis can be achieved. With a little luck one or two of them may provide a much better idea of where the better value is to be found and to whom the bride should now be talking seriously.

Even here, at this more committed stage, it is necessary to have two or three alternative suppliers. Between them and with them the bride should be developing final requirements in quite specific detail; the number of people to be catered for, the number of glasses of wine per head, the food menu if appropriate, etc., etc. Finally, the bride must shout "STOP!" when she has a professional view of what she believes she needs on the day and in good detail, something that she can live with and will not change and something to get serious about. This is the time to send for final quotations.

The requests for final quotations should be made in writing and in detail. Again, each of the favoured suppliers needs to receive exactly the same set of details to work with and if anything is changed at the suggestion of one, the others should be informed immediately. It must be made clear to each supplier that other suppliers are also being asked to provide final quotations but they must not learn of the companies they are quoting against. They should be given the impression that the decision will be based on value, not necessarily price alone.

When the quotations are received, a decision is then possible — easy as that! It never is, of course. The best price will be from the supplier least liked; the middle price means that those ugly, wooden, slatted chairs would be used, whereas the expensive price has elegant furniture, good food, etc., but is unaffordable! Whatever the decision, it will have been based on good sound planning and with even the least expensive of the quotations, the likelihood is that the bride is getting superior value and high standards. If this were not the case, the supplier would not have made it to the short list!

Reception

◆

Setting

When the ceremony is over the bride and groom will be able to relax and enjoy themselves with their guests. Feasts are a natural way of celebrating and allow both families to join in the festivities and get to know one another.

The choice of reception is the bride's and the groom's and may be a formal wedding breakfast, a buffet or a small dinner. The major considerations are the number of guests, the budget and the type of reception desired. Guests will spend some considerable time at the reception, so it is important to make the setting as comfortable as possible. For a sit-down meal, the guests will need somewhere to relax more informally so that they are free to mingle both before and after their meal. A buffet may also warrant the setting up of tables and chairs for all guests.

Catering is a vital consideration for any reception and choosing the right time, theme and venue helps to ensure that the celebrations are a success.

Timing

Some couples opt for a luncheon buffet, others prefer a more formal meal or cocktails and hors d'oeuvres. It should be borne in mind that the majority of guests will not enjoy a three hour midday party without lunch, or a meal served too early in the reception if people will have just eaten before they arrived.

Theme

A wedding may follow a particular theme such as Victorian or Scottish, in which case the reception menu should complement this.

Venue

Ideally the reception venue should be reasonably close to the church/register office or within a short and easy car journey.

Hotels

If finance is no problem, a hotel or restaurant reception means that all the catering arrangements, including staff, choice of menu and wine, can be organised and supplied by the management. A hotel can offer facilities for entertainment, accommodation for overnight guests, displays for wedding gifts, a comfortable place where the bride and groom can change and prepare themselves for their honeymoon, and should also be able to cope with the parking.

Hotels are possibly the most expensive option and on the minus side, they can be impersonal, numbers may be limited and time may be restricted.

When considering several hotel options, meals could be booked at the various venues to check the standard of food produced.

As soon as the venue is selected, a firm booking should be made and written confirmation obtained. Most hotels can only deal with one or two weddings in a day and consequently they may be booked well in advance.

Hall Hire

On a medium-sized budget, it should be possible to hire a local hall or a function room in a public house. However this option will require outside caterers.

Halls have the advantage of being able to accommodate large numbers, and they offer more freedom than a hotel. On the other hand, they can be bare and functional with limited facilities for catering. There may be few electric points, inadequate cooking and freezing facilities, poor work surfaces and water supply. There may also be insufficient furniture and inadequate toilet facilities and changing rooms for the bride and groom.

Almost certainly equipment such as crockery, cutlery and glassware will have to be hired, and the hall will need to be decorated. There may also be time restrictions.

Checklist 9 HOTEL

Hotel
 Venue _____
 Address _____
 _____
 _____
 Tel _____ Fax. _____
 Contact _____
Function
 Date _____ No. of guests: Adults _____
 Children _____
 Times Arival _____ Meal _____
 Speeches _____ Cake _____
 Entertainment _____
Facilities
 Room size ☐ _____ Changing room ☐
 Decor ☐ _____ Cloakroom/toilet ☐
 Heating ☐ _____ Gifts display ☐
 Seating ☐ _____ Car parking ☐
 Accommodation ☐
Food
 Supplier _____
 Cake _____
 Menu selected _____
 Special diets _____
 Servers _____
Drinks
 Provision ☐
 Licence to serve late ☐ _____
Equipment _____
Photographs _____
Confetti policy _____
Entertainment _____
Insurance
 Liability
 Gifts
Clearing away _____
£ _____

Checklist 10 **HALL**

Hall
  Venue _____
  Address _____
  _____
  _____
  _____
  _____
  Tel _____ Fax. _____
  Contact _____
Function   No. of guests   Adults _____
                                  Children _____
  Date _____
  Times Arrival _____
         Meal _____
         Speeches _____
         Cake _____
         Entertainment _____
Facilities
  Hall size
  Decorations
  Heating
  Seating arrangements
  Changing room
  Cloakroom and toilet facilities
  Gifts display
  Car parking
  Tables
  Food preparation facilities
  Drinks
Confetti policy _____
Entertainment _____
  Licence to serve late _____
Insurance _____
Clearing away _____
£ _____
Payment date _____

It is important to check the rules concerning the consumption of alcohol and to secure a written agreement for the booking, which should include details of all services to be provided.

Home

For a reception held at home, or at the home of a generous relative or friend, a buffet meal would probably be preferable, unless the number of guests is very small.

Home receptions have an intimate, comfortable and personal atmosphere, but the house would need to be sufficiently spacious to cater for a number of guests. Although home receptions do offer much freedom and timing is very flexible, numbers will inevitably be limited. Professional caterers should be booked well in advance.

A marquee in the garden offers maximum freedom and space, but, of course, the weather is always a problem, together with inadequate cloakroom, toilet and parking facilities.

Food

Meal Types

Meal options include: sit-down hot; sit-down cold (fork buffet); stand (finger buffet). Good food is vital to the success of a reception. It need not be exotic or extravagant but should be delicious, attractive and practical. A selection of well-chosen dishes to suit various tastes, and served attractively, will be much enjoyed.

A sit-down meal provides the opportunity to serve dishes such as soup and hot desserts. As everyone eats the same food, it is wise to choose 'safe' dishes that appeal to the majority. Chicken, turkey or beef are safe choices whereas liver, seafood and curry should be avoided.

If guests are to stand, a finger buffet is advisable. It is very difficult for guests to control food, plate, fork, glass and napkin while standing and trying to eat as well!

Guests may have special diets such as vegetarian or vegan, or they may need to avoid eating certain foods for other reasons such as allergy or religion. It is therefore necessary that such requirements are catered for when planning the menu.

Checklist 11 AT HOME

Function

No. of guests Adults _____ Children _____

Date _____

Time Arrival _____ Cake _____

Meal _____ Entertainment _____

Speeches _____

Facilities

Room space

Decorations

Heating

Tables

Chairs

Trestle tables for gifts display

Accommodation for overnight guests

Cloakroom and toilet facilities

Parking

Equipment

Crockery

Cutlery

Glassware

Cake stand and knife

Napkins

Candles

Table linen

Flower Arrangements

Food Cake

Menu

Special dietary requirements _____

Servers

Uniforms

Drink Barman

Wine waiter

Clearing away!

Entertainment

£ _____

Caterers

Outside Caterer
Professional caterers will suggest suitable menus for different budgets, provide linen, crockery, cutlery, silver, serve food and drinks, and clear up. Standards and prices vary and it is therefore advisable to compare their services and terms.

Self Catering
Self catering demands considerable effort and total commitment, for which ample time and appropriate temperament are essential. Capabilities and facilities must be realistically assessed as it is very easy to underestimate the amount of hard work involved.

It is wise not to be too ambitious but to keep things simple. Chores will need to be allocated and much assistance will be necessary for the day itself. A comprehensive timetable will provide invaluable help in the scheduling process. Carriage and transport to and from the venue is another important consideration.

Cocktails and hors d'oeuvres could be served in the afternoon as an alternative to a sit-down luncheon or dinner. A small dinner party for six to eight guests would be manageable, but for thirty a buffet would be more appropriate and is the simplest solution as much of the preparation can be done in advance of the wedding day. Food may be prepared and frozen in advance so that it is possible to concentrate on the fresh foods nearer the time.

Cake

The cake traditionally has pride of place on the top table, where it stands in the centre at a sit-down reception or in the centre of the food display table at a buffet.

Cutting
The cake-cutting ceremony traditionally concludes the formalities and follows the toasts, although it can take place beforehand so that slices may be cut for serving directly after the speeches.

Checklist 12 CATERER

Caterer

Name _____

Address _____

Tel _____ Fax _____

Qualifications _____

Experience _____

References _____

Capability to cope _____

Guests No: _____ Adults: _____ Children: _____

Function

Location _____

Date _____

Times _____ Arrival _____ Cake _____

Meal _____ Entertainment _____

Speeches _____ Close _____

Date booked with caterer: _____

Facilities

Room size _____

Furniture (tables, chairs, etc)_____

Decorations _____

Heating _____

Seating arrangements _____

Food preparation location _____

Cooking _____

Storage _____

Serving _____

Clearing up _____

Towels, etc. _____

Cloakroom/toilet _____

Toilet rolls _____

Soap _____

Staff changing _____

Parking _____

Checklist 12 **CATERER (cont.)**

Equipment
  Cutlery   _____
  Crockery   _____
  Glassware   _____
  Cake stand and knife   _____
  Table linen   _____
  Napkins   _____
  Candles   _____
  Flowers and table decor   _____
  Menu cards   _____
  Ashtrays   _____
  Tea, coffee pots   _____

Food
  Menu options   _____
  Menu selected   _____
    Hors d'oeuvres   _____
    Main course   _____
    Dessert   _____
    Cake cutting   _____
    Special dietary requirements   _____

Drink
  Alcoholic   _____
  Non-alcholic   _____

Staff
  Waiters   _____
  Waitresses   _____
  Wine servers   _____
  Barman   _____
  Uniforms   _____

Insurance
  Damages/breakages   _____

£   _____
Service, tips, VAT, deposit/cancellation. _____
Payment date(s)   _____

The first slice is ceremonially cut by the bride and groom with the groom's hand covering the bride's. Small slices are handed round on paper napkins so that they may be taken away by anyone not wishing to eat the cake at that time.

Cake Makers
It is wise to examine the literature and costs of more than one supplier. Some brides choose to make their own cake. The cake must be made at least four months in advance of the wedding.

Recipe
Traditionally, the cake is a classic rich fruit type with white royal icing piped and decorated.

Style
Styles include a single cake or a cake with several tiers. The latter is generally tiered with cakes of diminishing size - one on top of the other. The bottom or lower (larger) cakes are cut at the reception and the top layer kept for some future celebration such as a house warming, first wedding anniversary, or the christening of the first child.

Shape
There are numerous shapes from which to choose but the most popular are round or square.

Size
The supplier will advise on an appropriate size for the number of guests. Small slices are sent following the wedding to people who are unable to attend the reception.

Wedding cake is traditionally served in 2.5 cm (1″) square pieces.

Colour and Decorations
The most popular colour is white, but there is no reason why the colour should not complement the colour scheme of the wedding party or the flowers.

Royal icing is harder and easier to pipe, but fondant icing allows many different embellishments.

Checklist 13 **CAKE**

Supplier
  Name   _____
  Address   _____
  Tel   _____
  Contact   _____
Recipe   _____
Style   _____
Shape   _____
Size   _____ No. of guests _____
                                                 Extra _____
Colour   _____
Decorations   _____
                     Date _____ Time _____
Delivery / collection
  Delivery address_____

Cutting time   Before toasts   ☐ _____
                    or after toasts   ☐ _____

                            £ _____

Drink

The guests will naturally want liquid refreshments. If supplying drinks, quantities will depend on the number and thirst of the guests and a reasonable range should be provided, including a plentiful quantity of mixers, fresh fruit juices, soft drinks, and non-alcoholic wines.

Arrival at Reception
Traditionally, sherry is offered at this time. A medium and a dry provide an acceptable choice. An alternative could be to offer red and white wine.

Accompaniment to Meal
Wine is the customary drink to accompany the meal and the tradition of white wine with fish and red with most meats may no longer seem appropriate.

The Toasts
Champagne is traditional and there is now a range of types to suit various budgets. There are also less expensive alternatives to champagne, including sparkling white or rosé wines.

After the Meal
Very formal meals are sometimes followed by dessert wine, brandy, port or liqueurs. However, it is acceptable to serve tea and coffee and if there is a bar, guests may pay for their own drinks or a sum of money may be allocated so that they start paying when this is spent.

Seating Plan

A stand-up buffet-type reception demands no formal seating arrangements except that the bridal party should have a formal table where they can be served. Seats should be provided for the elderly and infirm and an area set aside for young children equipped with high chairs and a room where babies can be fed and changed.

For a formally seated reception, the top table is reserved for the wedding party. A table plan should be displayed to help guests find their seats quickly. This needs to be prepared in advance, along with the place name cards.

The seating of men and women should be alternated. Special circumstances, such as divorce, must be handled tactfully.

Top Table
The main bridal party sits along one side of a long table facing the guests, so that everyone can view the top table. The bride and groom sit in the middle; the groom on the right of the bride, and again men and women are alternated. Bridesmaids, page boys and ushers generally occupy seats on the other tables closest to the top table, or on the top table itself if space permits. A couple of examples:

Checklist 14 SEATING PLAN							
Chief brides-maid	Groom's father	Bride's mother	Groom	Bride	Bride's father	Groom's mother	Best man
Chief brides-maid	Bride's father	Bride's mother	Groom	Bride	Groom's father	Groom's mother	Best man

Remaining Tables

Closest relatives are usually seated nearest to the top table, after the attendants. Aunts, uncles and other relatives are next and then friends of the newly-weds. Layouts:

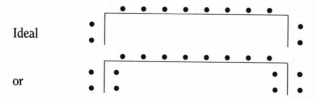

An alternative to these traditional arrangements is a room full of round tables which can provide a more relaxed atmosphere where guests are grouped tactfully with a good mix of men and women.

For an informal buffet, guests can only be expected to stand for a short time!

Entertainment

The style of music for the reception obviously depends on personal preference but a wise decision would be to have a selection of music that will allow everyone some enjoyment. Guests' ages may range from one to seventy which will demand plenty of variety. Besides ensuring that the music is acceptable to the majority, it can set the tone for the style of the reception; if everyone is expected to dance, plenty of dance music must be provided but if a quieter function is planned, then sophisticated background music may be a more suitable choice. Most people opt for a mixture of the two and assume that guests will want to talk first and start dancing later.

Musicians
There are many kinds of musicians from which to choose including steel bands, string quartets, singers, barbershop singers, jazz musicians, pianists and harpists.

For live music it should be possible to recruit a band that can provide variety by playing a little of everything — waltzes and gentle songs interspersed with lively dances. Performers can be found through recommendations from friends, hotel management or from the Yellow Pages. It can be advisable to listen to a taped performance or to attend a function at which the musicians are entertaining and to ensure that they are willing to perform the selections suitable for the atmosphere of the occasion.

The band will need to be informed of the kind of music desired, the frequency of particular pieces, any special requests that they may need to practise or learn in advance, the first dance as the bride and groom will dance to this alone, and any preferences for the last dance. Details such as the date, times, fees, provision of equipment and so on should be confirmed in writing.

Discothèque
Live bands are expensive and for this reason many couples choose a discothèque with a disc jockey who is capable of varying the entertainment to suit the guests. Many people prefer this option as 'discos' generally provide plenty of variety but as with bands, DJs all have their own personality and style so it is wise to choose someone in whom there is plenty of confidence. The selection of music will need to include waltzes and foxtrots as well as the more modern popular music. Most DJs who work regularly at weddings will have a varied up-to-date selection and

understand that music at weddings should not be too loud as guests will want to talk among themselves as well as join in the dancing.

Taped Music
To economize, music may be pre-recorded onto tape and a friend appointed to operate the equipment. A separate tape of background music may be useful during the meal and another, more lively, recording for the dancing later on.

Entertainer
For the children, a clown or a magician could be employed to entertain. Videos are another entertainment idea, particularly useful for keeping the younger generation fully occupied and happy.

Dancing

Traditionally, the bride and groom start the dancing with a slow number and dance alone for a few minutes. Then the best man and chief bridesmaid join in, followed by the two sets of parents. As the ushers and bridesmaids join them on the floor, they should encourage the guests to join in.

Sometime during the evening, the bride and groom whould dance with all the members of the wedding party of the opposite sex, and immediate family members; they should try to ensure that no one feels left out.

Leave Taking

At some stage during the reception, the bride slips away with her chief bridesmaid to change into her going-away outfit. This should be ready in a separate room somewhere convenient. The groom may also wish to change.

The bride may wish to have an informal leaving line whereby the guests line up with the men on one side and the ladies on the other. The bride thanks the men and the groom thanks the ladies.

Checklist 15 ENTERTAINMENT

Entertainer

Name _____

Address _____

_____

Tel _____

Venue

Address _____

Contact _____

Booking

Date _____

Time: Start _____   Finish _____

Music

First dance   Choice   Time

Special requests_____   _____

                 _____   _____

                 _____   _____

                 _____   _____

                 _____   _____

                 _____   _____

Equipment facilities _____

_____

_____

_____

                                          £_____

Deposit/cancellation _____

Payment date(s) _____

Honeymoon

A honeymoon is a chance to get away from it all, to wind down after the excitement of the wedding, to relax and enjoy each other's company.

The planning of a honeymoon is one of the most pleasant tasks of all the wedding arrangements. Obviously the type of holiday must be discussed between the couple in sufficient detail to allow the bride especially to pack suitable clothes.

Honeymoons are no longer luxuries afforded by only the rich; most couples take a break following their wedding and if the holiday coincides with the wedding plans it may be possible to have two or so weeks on a reasonable budget. All newly-married couples have one desire in common — to be on their own as much as possible. Considerations other than togetherness and finance availability for the venue, include the weather, climate, food, sport opportunities, activities and interests. This time may prove to be the ideal opportunity to visit some particular favoured destination that otherwise might not be possible. The choice should be made by the bride and groom according to personal preference, provisions of the budget with consideration for sensible forward planning of course and the amount of leave available.

For those who plan a honeymoon abroad and are restricted by limited finance, an ordinary package tour may be the solution. Popular destinations from this country include the Channel Islands, the Balearic Islands, Spain and Portugal, Malta, France, Greece, Italy, Germany, Austria and Switzerland.

For those who plan a honeymoon in this country, there are many attractive venues. A comparison of 'home and away' costs may be revealing; the cost of a week's hotel accommodation in Great Britain may amount to the same or more than self-catering abroad for a fortnight!

For those on a tight budget, many travel firms operate special honeymoon packages or bargain breaks and if the holiday is at an off-peak time, low season rates may apply. Reputable travel agents are members of

ABTA (Association of British Travel Agents) and are covered by their insurance bond should anything go wrong.

Arrangements and reservations should be made well in advance of the wedding day especially when travelling in high season to a popular holiday resort. Any necessary inoculations should be arranged as early as possible so that there is time to recover from any possible reactions.

The wedding day will be exhausting so it may be a good idea to stay in a nearby hotel for the first night, then journey on the honeymoon the following day.

Checklist 16   HONEYMOON

Departure time from reception	_____
Transport from reception	_____
First night details	_____
Honeymoon dates	From _____ To _____
Departure times	Out _____ In _____
Destination	_____
Return times	Out _____ In _____
Accommodation	
Name	_____
Address	_____
Tel	_____
Travel agent	
Name	_____
Address	_____
Tel	_____
Airport/station	_____
Flight/train no.	_____

Documentation

Passports	☐	Driving licences	☐
Marriage certificate	☐	Maps, etc.	☐
Currency and cheques	☐	Timetables	☐
Insurance	☐	_____	☐
Tickets	☐	_____	☐

Medical	
Inoculations	_____
Payment dates	_____

£

Duties

◆

Selecting Attendants

The bride's attendants may include a chief bridesmaid, bridesmaids and page boys. The groom is attended by a best man and ushers.

Family members are generally chosen as attendants and it is thoughtful to select from both families.

It is important that everyone knows both their own and everyone else's duties.

Checklist 17 **THE WEDDING PARTY WHO'S WHO**			
	Name	Address	Tel
Best man			
Chief bridesmaid			
Matron of honour			
Bridesmaid			
Bridesmaid			

Checklist 17 THE WEDDING PARTY WHO'S WHO (cont.)			
	Name	Address	Tel
Page boy			
Page boy			
Page boy			
Chief usher			
Usher			
Usher			
Bride's parents			
Groom's parents			

By tradition the bride's father is responsible for "giving the bride away", escorting her to church and up the aisle, and responding to the minister's question, "Who giveth this woman?" When the ceremony is over he should escort the groom's mother to the vestry, down the aisle and leave with her. If there is a formal wedding breakfast, he sits on the bride's left with the groom' mother next to him. The bride's father should be in formal dress if this is the choice of the groom and best man.

The responsibilities of the bride's mother are mainly the planning and preparations in close liaison with the bride as can be seen from the diary entries of duties in the following pages. In the ceremony however her role is minimal. Her place is in the front pew to the left of the aisle and at the conclusion of the ceremony she should walk with the groom's father into the vestry and kiss the bride immediately after the new husband. She leaves with the groom's father to take her place next to the bridal couple in the receiving line at the reception. If there is a formal breakfast, she sits on the right of the groom with his father on her right.

As the etiquette surrounding weddings has become less formal, so the duties of the bridesmaids, especially the chief bridesmaid, have tended to diminish from playing a very practical role in the bridal preparations to one of merely providing moral support for the bride. Chief bridesmaids are, for example, no longer necessarily expected to help the bride shop for her clothes or fetch and carry for her throughout the hectic pre-wedding weeks. It is still usual, however, for the chief bridesmaid to offer her assistance and to arrive at the bride's home in the early morning of the wedding day and help the bride to prepare. During the ceremony itself she is responsible for keeping a watchful eye on the child attendants if any. She leaves the church on the arm of the best man.

As will be seen from the following diary of specific duties of the best man, he has many duties to perform both during the preparations and on the day itself, his principal responsibilities being to ensure that the groom gets to the church on time, take charge of and hand over the ring at the appropriate time, give a speech and see that everyone is happy.

The following diary entries are based on having six months to plan the event and suggest how time may be organised.

The entries, some of which overlap, may be added to, deleted or adapted to suit individual needs and may be used to ensure that everything is covered.

Bride's Diary

6 months to go
- [ ] Announce news to parents
- [ ] Arrange for parents to meet and discuss specifics
- [ ] Inform relatives and close friends
- [ ] Have engagement party
- [ ] Arrange press announcements
- [ ] Draw up guest and gift list
- [ ] Compile budget
- [ ] Book ceremony venue
- [ ] Book reception venue, caterers, bar
- [ ] Order cake
- [ ] Appoint attendants
- [ ] Appoint helpers
- [ ] Discuss plans with attendants
- [ ] Book photographer/video
- [ ] Book transport
- [ ] Book entertainment
- [ ] Arrange passports

4 months to go
- [ ] Acquire attire for self and attendants
- [ ] Book florist
- [ ] Order stationery
- [ ] Plan honeymoon

2 months to go
- [ ] Acquire ring and gift for groom
- [ ] Ensure that gifts are bought for attendants
- [ ] Send invitations
- [ ] Circulate gift list
- [ ] Book hairdressing appointment
- [ ] Book beauty treatments
- [ ] Finalise arrangements for photographer
- [ ] Finalise arrangements for florist

- [ ] Check ceremony arrangements with groom
- [ ] Obtain licence
- [ ] Arrange overnight accommodation and transport for guests
- [ ] Have inoculations
- [ ] Write thank you letters for gifts as they arrive

1 month to go
- [ ] Have final dress fitting (bride and attendants)
- [ ] Finalise rehearsal arrangements
- [ ] Arrange pre-wedding parties
- [ ] Confirm guest numbers for reception
- [ ] Check honeymoon arrangements with groom
- [ ] Inform organisations of imminent change of marital status
- [ ] Submit announcements to the press

1 week to go
- [ ] Attend rehearsal and rehearsal party
- [ ] Ensure that all attendants know their duties
- [ ] Hold hen party
- [ ] Attend shower
- [ ] Arrange display of gifts
- [ ] Practise make-up and hair with headdress
- [ ] Confirm arrangements with all service suppliers
- [ ] Pack for honeymoon
- [ ] Arrange for return of hired items

1 day to go
- [ ] Relax

The day
- [ ] Arrive last at church
- [ ] Proceed up aisle supported on father's right arm followed by attendants
- [ ] Give bouquet and gloves to chief bridesmaid when at chancel steps
- [ ] Allow father or chief bridesmaid to lift veil ready for service
- [ ] Follow minister to sign register with groom

- ☐ Leave church with groom
- ☐ Pose for photographs
- ☐ Leave first for reception
- ☐ Greet guests with groom, after parents
- ☐ Enjoy meal
- ☐ Cut cake with groom
- ☐ Change into going-away outfit
- ☐ Toss bouquet or flowers

After honeymoon
- ☐ Write outstanding letters of thanks
- ☐ Order photographs
- ☐ Deal with documentation
- ☐ Ensure that slices of cake have been sent
- ☐ Arrange press report
- ☐ Entertain both sets of parents

It is impossible to be too specific about planning since this obviously depends on many factors, such as the type of ceremonies, the style of reception and the fact that everyone has different methods of dealing with a procedure. However, most brides would agree that the earlier the planning the better.

It will be obvious from the diaries, that the bride and her mother need to work together closely throughout the planning stages.

Groom's Diary

6 months to go
- [ ] Announce news to parents
- [ ] Arrange for parents to meet and discuss specifics
- [ ] Inform relatives and close friends
- [ ] Have engagement party
- [ ] Draw up guest list with bride
- [ ] Compile budget with bride
- [ ] Book ceremony venue with bride
- [ ] Appoint best man and ushers with bride
- [ ] Book reception venue, caterers, bar with bride
- [ ] Appoint helpers with bride
- [ ] Discuss plans with attendants
- [ ] Plan attire for self and other male members of the wedding party
- [ ] Check legal details of wedding
- [ ] Inform best man of seating arrangements for church and reception

4 months to go
- [ ] Acquire outfit
- [ ] Book and settle honeymoon
- [ ] Arrange passports and travellers' cheques

2 months to go
- [ ] Acquire ring and gifts for bride, best man, bridesmaids, page boys and ushers
- [ ] Arrange and pay for transport
- [ ] Pay for flowers for bride and attendants
- [ ] Write speech
- [ ] Check ceremony arrangements with bride
- [ ] Obtain licence

1 month to go
- [ ] Finalise rehearsal arrangements with bride
- [ ] Arrange stag night
- [ ] Buy ribbons for cars

1 week to go

- ☐ Attend rehearsal, rehearsal party and pass on gifts
- ☐ Ensure that attendants know their duties
- ☐ Have hair cut
- ☐ Hold stag night
- ☐ Pack for honeymoon
- ☐ Arrange for return of hired items

1 day to go

- ☐ Relax

The day

- ☐ Ensure that luggage and going-away outfit are at the reception
- ☐ Ensure that going-away car is at reception
- ☐ Give church fees to best man
- ☐ Arrive at church with best man
- ☐ Step up to altar when bride arrives
- ☐ Follow minister to sign register with bride
- ☐ Leave church with bride
- ☐ Pose for photographs
- ☐ Leave first for reception
- ☐ Greet guests with bride, after parents
- ☐ Give speech and propose toast to the bridesmaids
- ☐ Cut cake with bride
- ☐ Change into going-away outfit
- ☐ Collect documentation from best man

After honeymoon

- ☐ Pay to best man out-of-pocket expenses
- ☐ Entertain both sets of parents

Bridesmaids' Duties

A bridesmaid is an unmarried attendant whose role is to help the bride whenever needed. A widow remarrying would not be accompanied by bridesmaids but by a matron of honour.

(The bride arranges outfits)
- ☐ Help with bride's dress before and after ceremony
- ☐ Get into car destined for the ceremony, leaving the bride alone with mother and giver-away for a few minutes
- ☐ Look after wedding attire
- ☐ Carry comb and pocket mirror for use by the bride
- ☐ Follow the chief bridesmaid up the aisle
- ☐ Wait at chancel steps or sit as instructed
- ☐ Follow chief bridesmaid and best man out of the church after the register is signed
- ☐ Leave for the reception with the chief bridesmaid and best man after the bride and groom and after the photographs
- ☐ Offer drinks to guests at reception (older bridesmaids only)
- ☐ Distribute slices of cake
- ☐ Wear dresses and head-dresses all day and evening

Flower Girl

A flower girl is a very young child whose role could be purely decorative in that she will add some visual advantage to the attendants and she could precede the bride down the aisle scattering flower petals or confetti, if allowed.

Page Boys' Duties

(Bride arranges outfits)
- ☐ Follow chief bridesmaid up the aisle
- ☐ Wait at chancel steps or sit as instructed
- ☐ Follow chief bridesmaid and best man out of church
- ☐ Leave for the reception with chief bridesmaid and best man after the bride and groom
- ☐ Distribute slices of cake
- ☐ Behave!

Chief Bridesmaid/Matron of Honour's Diary

Since the chief bridesmaid acts as adviser, messenger and general assistant to the bride, she is usually an unmarried sister or an unmarried close friend.

A matron of honour is a married lady attendant. She is sometimes chosen instead of bridesmaids when she will be the sole attendant acting as chief and only bridesmaid. Her duties are those of a chief bridesmaid but she will not usually wear the finery.

The duties of the chief bridesmaid involve assisting the bride as much as possible with the wedding planning and preparations, attending the pre-wedding festivities, and on the day, ensuring that the bride looks her best. She will be near to the bride throughout the proceedings and is the equivalent of the groom's best man. Her responsibilities include marshalling and taking charge of the young attendants — specially taking care of any younger bridesmaids. At the reception she may join the receiving line and can be generally helpful in circulating with the guests. When it is time to leave she will help the bride to change and will usually look after the wedding dress.

4 months to go

- ☐ Arrange and pay for own outfit unless it is unsuitable for wear at other occasions
- ☐ Help the bride to choose bridesmaids' dresses
- ☐ Discuss plans with bride, groom and best man
- ☐ Offer to babysit youngsters, while bride and her mother run wedding errands
- ☐ Attend pre-wedding parties and rehearsal

The day

- ☐ Ensure that bouquets are ready for the bride and bridesmaids
- ☐ Help bride to dress and make-up ready for the ceremony
- ☐ Ensure that bridesmaids arrive promptly
- ☐ Carry emergency supplies: tissues, comb, make-up, hairclips, safety pins, etc.

- ☐ Leave for the church with the other bridesmaids and bride's mother
- ☐ Marshall the bridesmaids and pages
- ☐ Assemble with bridesmaids and pages in the church porch
- ☐ Arrange bride's dress, veil and train
- ☐ Take charge of the bride's bouquet and gloves at chancel steps
- ☐ Ensure that bride's veil is lifted
- ☐ Accompany best man into the vestry, following the bride and groom
- ☐ Sign register if called upon to do so
- ☐ Return bouquet and gloves to the bride in the vestry
- ☐ Leave church with the best man after the bride and groom
- ☐ Pose for photographs
- ☐ Leave for the reception with the best man and other bridesmaids after the bride and groom

At reception
- ☐ Form part of the receiving line and greet guests
- ☐ Help to display and record gifts received
- ☐ Offer drinks to guests
- ☐ Look after bride's bouquet
- ☐ Check that bride's going-away outfit is ready
- ☐ Help bride to change into her going-away outfit
- ☐ Take charge of bride's dress
- ☐ Check that bride's luggage is ready
- ☐ Retrieve bouquet and hand to bride when she is about to leave
- ☐ See bride to the car

After the wedding
- ☐ Return own and bride's outfits if hired

Bridesmaids' Mothers' Duties

The bridesmaids' mothers traditionally pay for the bridesmaids' attire.

Best Man

The best man is the groom's assistant and is usually his brother or a close friend chosen by the groom.

Qualities
The best man needs to be level-headed, confident in a crisis and a diplomat all rolled into one. He must be well-informed of all of the preparations and procedures for the day and should not be left to make vague guesses as to requirements. An element of common sense is essential and as he is responsible for the groom's time-keeping, punctuality is very important. To do a good job, the best man needs to be capable of remaining sober. As an all-round helper, observation and tact are essential to smooth operations. The speech is probably the part dreaded most, but although a good speech is important, no one expects a polished, witty professional performance.

Someone who is born to be a superb best man is a rare commodity and yet people are doing a great job in this role every day!

Preparation is the key to performing the duties and acquiring all the qualities of the perfect best man. In his role as organiser, he should be relied upon to handle the duties delegated to him.

Responsibilities
The best man's major responsibility is to ensure that the groom gets to the church on time. He must also make a speech at the reception, respond to the toast to the bridesmaids, read the telegrams/telemessages, organise the ushers, take care of the ring(s), documentation and fees and arrange the stag night in consultation with the groom.

The best man generally supports the groom through the preparation and the trials of the day itself.

It is a great honour to be asked to be best man; it is a vote of the groom's friendship and confidence. But the groom should remember that the job of best man should give his friend pleasure!

Checklist 18   BEST MAN'S FACT FILE

Date of wedding _____

Ceremony
  Venue _____
  Arrival time for groom _____
  Name of minister/registrar _____
  Tel _____
  Time that fees are payable _____
  Confetti rules _____
  Photos/videos restrictions _____
  Parking arrangements _____

Attire
  Groom _____
  Best man _____
  Accessories _____

Hire firm
  Name _____
  Address _____
  Tel _____
  Fitting date(s) _____
  Collection date(s) _____
  Return date(s) _____

Flowers
  Buttonholes _____
  Corsages _____

Rehearsal
  Date _____
  Time _____

Stag Night
  Date _____
  Time _____
  Transport _____

Photographers appointed
  Name _____
  Tel _____
  Emergency
  Name _____ Tel _____

Checklist 18 BEST MAN'S FACT FILE (cont.)

Reception
Venue _____
Contact _____
Tel _____
Time _____
Parking facilities _____
No. of guests _____
Toastmaster _____
Seating plan _____
Meal _____
   Time _____
   Arrangements _____
   Speech time _____
   People to thank _____
Bar facilities _____
Entertainment _____
Changing room for bride and groom _____
Leaving time _____
Departure details _____
Transport
To Church
   Groom and Best Man _____
   Parking facilities _____
To Reception
   Bride and Groom _____
   Bridesmaids, etc. _____
   Parents _____
   Guests _____
   Parking facilities _____
To Honeymoon
   Bride and Groom _____
Car hire
Firm _____
Address _____
Cars to be supplied _____
Collection/delivery time _____ Tel _____

Checklist 18   BEST MAN'S FACT FILE (cont.)

Taxi
  Firm _____
  Address _____
  Tel _____
Emergency firm
  Name _____
  Address _____
  Tel _____

Checklist 18   BEST MAN'S FACT FILE (cont.)

	Name	Address	Tel
WHO'S WHO Bride			
Groom			
Chief bridesmaid/ Matron of honour			
Bridesmaid			
Bridesmaid			
Flower girl			
Page boy			

Checklist 18	BEST MAN'S FACT FILE (cont.)		
	Name	Address	Tel
WHO'S WHO Page boy			
Page boy			
Chief Usher			
Usher			
Usher			
Bride's parents			
Groom's parents			

Best Man's Diary

The morning of the wedding will be busy for the best man as there are some things which cannot be done in advance. It is therefore important to deal with as much as possible prior to the day of the wedding.

6 months to go
- ☐ Send written reply immediately on receipt of invitation
- ☐ Book date in diary
- ☐ Cancel other engagements

3 months to go
- ☐ Discuss plans with the bride, groom and chief bridesmaid and make notes
- ☐ Help to choose the ushers
- ☐ Help with the wedding preparations

2 months to go
- ☐ Consult the wedding gift list and purchase special gift
- ☐ Arrange and pay for own outfit
- ☐ Check that groom and ushers have organised their own outfits
- ☐ Help to choose groom's and ushers' clothes and accessories, if desired
- ☐ Prepare and draft speech
- ☐ Practise and time the speech
- ☐ Compile a list of close family
- ☐ Pass this list to ushers to help them with seating arrangements at the church
- ☐ Liaise with ushers and instruct them on their duties and timing
- ☐ Visit the reception venue with bride and groom, to check parking, times, etc.
- ☐ Remind groom to check passports, order travellers' cheques and to have inoculations, etc.

6 weeks to go
- [ ] Organise stag party
- [ ] Book stag night venue
- [ ] Check licence/banns arrangements have been made

1 month to go
- [ ] Check that buttonholes have been ordered
- [ ] Check that honeymoon arrangements have been made
- [ ] Check routes to groom's home, to church and to the reception by doing test runs
- [ ] Arrange transport for groom and self to church, to reception, going-away vehicle for newly weds and own transport from reception
- [ ] Arrange car service if appropriate
- [ ] Purchase car decorations

2 weeks to go
- [ ] Finalise speech and write prompt cards
- [ ] Check parking arrangements at church and reception
- [ ] Deputise ushers to assist with parking
- [ ] Purchase phonecard

1 week to go
- [ ] Attend rehearsal
- [ ] Hand over gift to bride and groom
- [ ] Check licence/banns certificate is collected
- [ ] Purchase a spare ring
- [ ] Collect order of service sheets
- [ ] Ensure groom's safety at and after stag night

2 days to go
- [ ] Check and confirm transport arrangements

1 day to go
- [ ] Collect hired attire
- [ ] Check buttonholes
- [ ] Ensure luggage is packed
- [ ] Check car

The day
- [ ] Check that groom is ready
- [ ] Check transport
- [ ] Check ushers
- [ ] Collect buttonholes
- [ ] Check with bride's parents
- [ ] Collect telegrams
- [ ] Supervise the ushers
- [ ] Check groom's luggage
- [ ] Check groom's change of clothes
- [ ] Help groom to prepare
- [ ] Place ring(s) in a safe pocket
- [ ] Have church fees ready
- [ ] Keep documentation safe
- [ ] Set off for church early
- [ ] Accompany the groom to church

At church
- [ ] Check on ushers
- [ ] Pay church fees
- [ ] Pose for photographs outside the church
- [ ] Take seat in the front pew on the right side of church
- [ ] Take charge of groom's hat and gloves
- [ ] Wait on the right side of and a little behind the groom at the ceremony
- [ ] Move forward with the groom to stand in front of the steps
- [ ] Hand over the ring(s)
- [ ] Escort the chief bridesmaid to the vestry
- [ ] Sign register if called upon to do so
- [ ] Escort chief bridesmaid out of the church following the bride and groom

☐ Escort newly-weds to the photographer
☐ Escort the guests to their cars
☐ Leave for reception with bridesmaids after bride and groom

At reception

☐ Join the end of the receiving line or announce the guests
☐ Take charge of late wedding gifts
☐ Collect and vet the telegrams/telemessages
☐ Offer drinks to guests
☐ Guide guests to seating plan
☐ Escort guests to their seats
☐ Request silence for grace
☐ Enjoy meal
☐ Call on speakers
☐ Reply on behalf of the bridesmaids, give speech and read telegrams
☐ Dance with female attendants and guests
☐ Deal with newly-weds' luggage
☐ Hand over documentation
☐ Help to clear up

After wedding

☐ Check that gifts are carefully stored
☐ Return hired attire
☐ Write thank you note for gift

Ushers' Diaries

Ushers form the best man's team of helpers. They are traditionally unmarried and are usually brothers or close relatives of the bride and groom. Ushers are chosen by the groom in consultation with the best man.

Traditionally there are as many ushers as there are bridesmaids so that they may escort the bridesmaids during the course of the day. However, since escorts are no longer considered essential, this particular custom is not always strictly followed, but it is thoughtful if ushers can ensure that the bridesmaids are looked after during the day.

The responsibilities of an usher are not onerous but if the job is done well, it helps the smooth running of the wedding day and takes care of several minor worries of those principally involved in the organising.

Traditionally, the best man is in charge of the ushers and he ensures that they know their duties, are properly dressed, and are in the right place at the right time.

3 months to go
☐ Receive from the best man a list of close family to help with seating arrangements
☐ Liaise with the best man about arrangements
☐ Arrange and pay for own outfit and accessories including a large black umbrella!

2 weeks to go
☐ Have hair cut
☐ Liaise with other ushers
☐ Confirm arrival time at church

The day
☐ Carry umbrella
☐ Escort bridesmaids during the day
☐ Collect and distribute buttonholes
☐ Collect order of service sheets from best man

- ☐ Arrive first at church
- ☐ Organise car parking
- ☐ Allocate buttonholes and corsages to principal guests
- ☐ Line up on left side of entrance
- ☐ Greet guests and hand out hymn books, prayer books and/or order of service sheets
- ☐ Inform guests of restrictions regarding photographs and confetti
- ☐ Escort guests to pews: bride's family on the left; groom's on the right
- ☐ Take own seat

After the ceremony
- ☐ Direct guests to the venue for photographs
- ☐ Ensure that all guests have transport to the reception
- ☐ Direct guests to the reception venue
- ☐ Ensure that the church is left tidy
- ☐ Clean up confetti

At reception
- ☐ Offer drinks to guests as they arrive
- ☐ Introduce people to one another
- ☐ Look after elderly or infirm guests
- ☐ Dance with as many guests as possible

After wedding
- ☐ Return hired attire
- ☐ Send thank you note for gift to bride and groom

Checklist 19	USHER'S FACT FILE		
Role and specifc duties	Name	Address	Tel
Best man (supervises ushers)			
Chief usher			
Usher 2			
Usher 3			
Usher 4			

Giver-away's Diary

The giver-away is usually the bride's father, but can be a brother, male guardian, relative or other male.

Before the wedding
☐ Ask the minister to say grace at the reception but if he is not attending, prepare grace
☐ Arrange wedding attire
☐ Write speech

The day
☐ Escort the bride from home to church

At church
☐ Arrive last with bride
☐ Lead procession to chancel steps with the bride on right arm
☐ Take bride's right hand and give to the minister at the appropriate time
☐ Give away the bride
☐ Accompany the groom's mother to the vestry after the service, followed by the best man and chief bridesmaid
☐ Leave the church with the groom's mother
☐ Pose for photographs
☐ Leave for the reception with other parents after the best man and bridesmaids

At reception
☐ Arrive first at the reception venue with the bride's mother to host the reception
☐ Form part of the reception line and greet the guests with bride's mother
☐ Say grace if minister is absent
☐ Indicate to the waitresses that the meal may start
☐ Propose the toast of the bride and groom if called upon to do so by the best man
☐ Pay for the reception!

Bride's Mother's Diary

The bride's mother puts in all her hard work beforehand and behind the scenes. She will have done most of the work arranging the reception and will have supervised the sending of the invitations and so on, not forgetting the help and advice she will have given to the bride concerning wedding attire and trousseau.

The bride's mother acts as hostess of the wedding and helps in all aspects of the planning arrangements.

Before the wedding
- ☐ Arrange outfit and accessories
- ☐ Draw up guest list with bride and groom's family
- ☐ Arrange press announcements
- ☐ Order stationery
- ☐ Send out the invitations and list responses
- ☐ Display gifts at home
- ☐ Organise flowers with bride
- ☐ Order transport with bride
- ☐ Order cake
- ☐ Arrange for a photographer with bride
- ☐ Arrange reception and entertainment with bride

The day
- ☐ Help bride to dress and fix veil
- ☐ Travel to church with bridesmaids
- ☐ Arrive at church before the bride
- ☐ Sit in the front pew on the left of the aisle
- ☐ Make way to vestry with groom's father to sign the register
- ☐ Leave the church on the left arm of the groom's father following the bridesmaids and page boys
- ☐ Pose for photographs
- ☐ Leave for the reception

At reception
- ☐ Act as hostess
- ☐ Form the receiving line and greet guests with the bride's father
- ☐ Give signal to best man for meal to begin
- ☐ Leave last

After wedding
- ☐ Send slices of cake to those who were unable to attend the wedding
- ☐ Organise photograph proofs and collect orders for photographer

Parents

Usually, both sets of parents cooperate in the arrangements and the finances.

The bride's parents usually host the wedding (as they are generally responsible for the majority of the expenses involved) and help in all aspects of the planning and arrangements. They are responsible for sending out the invitations and receiving the replies. Wedding gifts are usually sent to their home prior to the wedding date, where they are displayed for callers to view. As host and hostess, they are first in the receiving line at the reception and are usually responsible for ensuring that all guests leave safely and that the clearing up is attended to.

By comparison, the groom's family have little to do, although they should be consulted about the venue of the ceremony and the reception. The groom's parents sit at the front of the church on the right and join the wedding party when they go to sign the register. They usually join the receiving line at the reception to greet the guests as they arrive.

Speeches and Toasts

Speeches include the toasts and usually occur after the meal. They are followed by the cutting of the cake ceremony.

The delivery of speeches and toasts is the part of the day that many people dread the most, but with a little planning and careful preparation, it really need not be an ordeal.

Every speechmaker is nervous, but it is not difficult to make a wedding speech as the audience is already warmed by the happiness of the occasion and they do not expect nor want a long and important serious oratory! They simply expect a few sincere and perhaps amusing words so that they can get on with the occasion.

Following each toast, all guests should stand, raise their glasses, repeat the toast and drink to whoever is mentioned.

Second Marriages
At a second marriage the toast to the bride and groom may still be proposed by the bride's father, but this is fairly unusual. This toast would normally be proposed by a male friend.

Order of Toasts
Each speaker should be announced briefly by the toastmaster or the best man.

First Toast
The giver-away stands and says a few words about the bride and groom before proposing the toast to the health of the bride and groom.

Reply
The groom responds on behalf of the bride and himself.

Second Toast
The groom proposes a toast to the bridesmaids.

Reply
The best man replies on behalf of the bridesmaids and reads the telegrams.

Planning
There are three ways of presenting a speech:
— read from notes;
— recite from memory;
— refer to brief 'headline' note cards (memory-joggers) from previously planned text.

The first method is disastrous! The second option is inflexible. The best method is the third in that the main points will not be forgotten, the speech will have shape and possesses the flexibility for improvisation.

Postcard-sized cards should state a separate word or phrase followed by a few memory-jogging notes. Cards also have the advantage of providing something to do with hands!

Practise
A mirror, a tape recorder or a video, and a watch will be invaluable when practising.

Presentation
The aim is to appear confident with an easy relaxed manner. Deep breaths help considerably.

Speech Manner
It is important not to sound pompous and/or patronising but on the other hand, too much informality must be avoided.

Slang and Swearing
Slang detracts from the 'sense of occasion'. The speaker must never swear!

Pronunciation
A natural accent is recommended.

Voice Level
A speaker's voice simply must be heard or there is no point making a speech at all.

Duration
Speeches must be brief and should take no longer than five minutes.

Pace
The speaker must remember to breathe! The best advice is to speak slowly and clearly, pausing between sentences or even between phrases.

Posture
The speaker should position his feet slightly apart and stand upright but relaxed.

Gestures
Unless gestures come naturally when illustrating speech, these should be avoided.

Vision
The speaker should look in the general direction of the audience and towards the subject of the toast when proposing.

Content
Like every properly constructed speech, a wedding speech must have a beginning, a middle and an end. Wording for the toasts at the end of speeches may be: *'I ask you to rise and drink the health of ...'*, for example.

A response to the toast need not be quite so formal, but it must be made clear in the opening sentence that the speaker is thanking the company for drinking the speaker's health. A simple *'Thank you very much ...'* is often effective, or *'I (or we) thank you most sincerely for your kind wishes.'* To conclude the speech, it is acceptable to repeat the thanks for the toast that has been drunk.

Jokes and Comic Stories
Making jokes at other people's expense is unforgivable, yet making jokes at one's own expense is acceptable. Vulgar and even risqué jokes or stories must be avoided.

Quotations

Quotations can form part of a speech as a source of an idea - used as an introduction to a story for example. Like jokes, they may be adapted to suit the circumstances and can add purpose and shape to a speech. More than two quotations can sound awfully pompous, but one or two can be useful to start a train of thought which makes the whole thread of a speech particularly if there is one that is especially apt to the circumstances of the wedding. Many quotations are not very flattering about the institution of marriage — indeed some are positively cynical — and it is obvious that many writers had jaded views so it is important that speakers choose something that will not offend; if the more jaded views are voiced they must be qualified by a denial of the truth of their sentiments, for example, "Anyone would find it impossible to hold such views in the presence of such obvious wedded happiness".

The Bride's Speech

There is really no need for the bride to make a speech and she is seldom expected to do so. However, the custom is growing for the bride to say a few words if she wishes — three or four sentences to thank her husband are sufficient but she may make a longer speech if she feels up to it.

The best man would normally introduce the bride. Sometimes, the bride speaks immediately after her husband has responded to the toast to the two of them, but if he is proposing the toast to the bridesmaids, this is difficult as he has to rise again after the bride to propose the toast. Consequently this is not really satisfactory and to remedy the situation, it is better that someone else proposes the toast to the bridesmaids. If the bride decides to make a speech, the order of speakers will need careful consideration in advance.

Telegrams/Telemessages

Guests who are unable to attend the wedding should write to the bride's parents expressing regret and perhaps send a card. If the guest is a close friend of either the bride or groom, they should also send another note (informally written) to the couple.

A greeting telegram timed to arrive on the wedding day is a good way of conveying best wishes and may be informal. The reading out of wittily composed telegrams can add gaiety to a wedding reception; however, messages should be vetted prior to their reading and anything unsuitable discarded. If there are many telegrams, the best man should make a selection, otherwise the guests will become bored very quickly. All those with the same or similar message such as 'Best Wishes' can be grouped together and the greeing mentioned only once. The bride should advise the best man beforehand so that he is aware of any messages which she would specifically like included.

Checklist 20 SPEECHES	✔
Plan speech	
Be brief (3 minutes — 5 minutes)	
Do not use long words	
Do not use formal phrases not normally used	
Do not swear or use slang	
Be to the point	
Be sincere	
Avoid embarrassing stories	
Be careful of telling jokes	
Write prompt cards	
Ensure that there is a glass of water at hand	
Limit the number of drinks before the speech	
Rehearse speech	
Stand still but relaxed	
Take deep breaths	
Stick to the plan	
Look at the audience as you speak but do not stare	
Speak slowly, audibly and clearly	
Keep the tone conversational	
Propose or respond to the toast	

Guest List

◆ ◆ ◆

Draft List

Preparing a guest list can be contentious as it may not be possible to invite everyone. Great tact is vital if resentment is to be avoided.

Traditionally, the bride's mother compiles the guest list in consultation with the groom's family but today the decision largely rests with the person who pays the bill!

The guest list, when finalised, may also be used for recording gifts from guests and will be useful when writing thank-yous, as addresses will be readily available.

Final List

Checks will need to be made on any special needs, for example vegetarian diets, high-chairs, wheelchairs.

Checklist 21 GUEST AND GIFT RECORD		
TOTAL NUMBERS		Invited
	Adults _____	
	Children _____	
Name	**Address**	**Telephone No.**

Accepted

_____

_____

Defi-nite	Prob-able	Possi-ble	Invita-tion sent	Special needs	Gift rec'd	Thank-you note sent (Date)

Announcements and Printing

◆◆◆

Details about engagement announcements are contained in Chapter 2.

The Press

In much the same way as for engagements, many couples like to announce their wedding in the local paper so that casual friends may join in wishing them well at the church or register office, or send them a card, for example.

Letters of Announcement

If there are people whom the couple would particularly like informed about their marriage, but because the limitations of the guest list has meant that they cannot be invited to the wedding, a personal letter is probably the best way to let them know the news.

Personal Letters of Invitation

Before the formal invitations are despatched, relatives and close friends may be informed by personal letter, the wording of which could be as follows:

"You will be glad to hear that Nel and Sam's wedding has been arranged for 2 May. We shall, of course, be sending you a formal invitation later, but we felt sure you would be delighted to have the news as soon as possible."

Formal Invitations

About four months before the wedding, invitations should be ordered and despatched to the guests named on the guest list, having been finalised in consultation with the groom's parents. They are traditionally from and sent by the bride's parents (usually the mother), as they generally host the occasion, indicating their responsibility for the payment of the reception. But if the wedding is being hosted by anyone else, such as the bride and groom themselves, then they should assume this task.

Style
The style of invitations can be an indication of the style of wedding. There are many styles from which to choose and about which the local stationers and printers can advise.

Ordering
Each couple or each family needs only one invitation, although teenagers over eighteen should receive their own invitations even if they live with their parents.

Wording
Traditionally, an invitation is addressed to the wife of a couple or family. The addressees' names are normally handwritten in the top left-hand corner if they do not form part of the main wording. The bride's surname is not normally included but it can be appropriate if different from that of the host and hostess. The wording must be perfectly clear and free from ambiguity.

Enclosures
Unless everyone is local, it can be useful to enclose a map of the area with the invitations.

Example wording for a wedding given by bride's parents

> Mr and Mrs N/Ned North
> request the pleasure of your company/
> request the company of
> ...
> at the marriage of their daughter
> Nel
> to/with
> Mr Sam South
> at St Mark's Church, Northton
> on Saturday 2 May 19-- at 2.30 pm
> and at the reception afterwards
> at Stone Manor, Northton
>
> RSVP
> (Address)

Replies to Invitations

Formal invitations require formal replies and should be sent within three days of receipt so that it is possible to have a definite idea of numbers. Acceptances and refusals should be entered on the guest and gifts record as they are received.

Order of Service Sheets

Pre-printed order-of-service sheets enable the congregation to follow the service and hymns without referring back and forth from prayer book to hymn book. The minister must be consulted before bulk printing is authorised to ensure that all elements are correct.

The best man passes the sheets onto the chief usher, who ensures that one of the ushers distributes them to the guests as they arrive at church.

Menus

If there is a choice of fare, menu cards may be printed for the guests.

Place Name Cards

Place name cards are useful so that the guests know where to sit at the reception.

Seating Plan

An overall seating plan enables guests to know the general location of their seats as they enter the dining room.

Compliments Cards and Cake Boxes

Compliments cards are despatched with cake slices to those who were unable to attend on the day. Attractive cake boxes are used to despatch the cake through the post.

Guest Book

A book for guests to sign at the reception can provide a memorable keepsake.

Other Stationery and Souvenirs

Many items such as napkins, napkin rings, drink mats, etc. may be monogrammed and kept as souvenirs.

Thank-you Cards and Letters

Thank you cards and letters can be pre-printed with standard text or they may be personally handwritten.

Desk Diary

A desk diary is a good investment to aid planning.

Post-wedding News

Many couples arrange a press report of the wedding to appear in the local newspaper.

Checklist 22 **PRINTING**				
	Invitations	Order of service sheets	Thank yous	Other
Supplier				
Address				
Tel				
Fax				
No. required				
Style				
Size				
Paper/card				
Paper/card colour				
Print style				
Print colour				
Wording/ Monogram				
£				

Photography and Video

◆◆◆

The photographer's skill can create the most important memento of all.

Photographer

Most brides would recommend that a professional is employed for the occasion. An assessment of a photographer's experience can be checked by examination of previous work. Most photographers offer a wedding package but these do vary. In many cases there is a standard fee which includes attendance at the wedding to take a certain number of photographs. A deposit will be necessary when booking a photographer. After the wedding day, he will print proofs of all the shots for the bride and groom to choose.

Checklist 23 **PHOTOGRAPHER**

Photographer _____

Address _____

Tel _____

When was the firm established? _____

Do they specialise in weddings? ☐ _____

Package details _____

Attendance fee _____

Set number of prints _____

Is the cost of the album included? ☐ _____

Who keeps the proofs? _____

When will the proofs be ready? _____

How long may the proofs be retained? _____

When will the photographs be ready? _____

£ each finished photograph _____

£ additional albums _____

£ additional individual photos _____

When do prices increase? _____

Deposit/cancellation arrangements ☐ _____

Please confirm all points in writing ☐ _____

Double check date and times nearer the date ☐ _____

£ _____

The Photographs

It is important to check whether photographs are allowed inside the church or register office. Some ministers allow photographs as long as no flashes or flood lights are used whilst others may allow photographs as long as these are not taken during the actual marriage itself. Some photographers do not automatically attend the reception but this can be arranged or perhaps a friend can oblige.

The following list may be used to agree with the photographer the shots particularly wanted.

Checklist 24   PHOTOGRAPHS

Wedding date _____

Meeting dates _____

	Time	Type of shot
At home before the ceremony		
Address _____		
Close up		
With mother		
With father		
With mother and father		
With family		
With attendants		
At gift table		
Full length		
Adjusting veil		
With flowers		
At dressing table		
Bride putting on her veil		
Bridesmaids getting ready		
In the garden		
Mother and attendants leaving		
Leaving with father		
At the ceremony		
Location _____		
Arrival of: guests		
groom and best man		
Groom		
Groom with best man		
Groom with ushers		
Arrival of: bridesmaids,		
page boys		
and bride's mother		
bride and giver-away		

Checklist 24 PHOTOGRAPHS (cont.)

	Time	Type of shot
Bridesmaids		
Page boys		
Bride outside church		
Ushers		
Wedding party assembled		
During the ceremony		
(if allowed)		
In church		
Bride going down the aisle		
The marriage itself		
(if allowed)		
In the vestry for the		
signing of the register		
Leaving the church		
At the church door,		
bride & groom together		
After the ceremony		
Leaving the church		
Bride and groom at the church door		
Outside the church/register office		
Bride and groom together		
Couple with best man, bridesmaids		
and other attendants		
All attendants together		
Couple with bride's family		
Couple with groom's family		
Couple with both sets of parents		
Couple getting into the car		
Outside the church/register office		

Checklist 24   PHOTOGRAPHS (cont.)

		Time	Type of shot
Formal after ceremony shots			
Exact location _____			
Bride	Alone		
	With bridesmaids		
	With bride's parents		
Bride and groom	Together		
	With bride's parents		
	With groom's parents		
	With both sets of parents		
	With parents, best man and bridesmaids		
	With bride's family		
	With groom's family		
	With friends		
	With guests throwing rice, etc.		
	Leaving for reception		
	In car		
At the reception			
Location _____			
Bride and groom arriving			
Receiving guests			
With bride's parents			
With groom's parents			
With both sets of parents			
With special friends			
With godparents			
The tables			
Proposing toasts			
During toasts and speeches			
Cutting of the cake			

Checklist 24 PHOTOGRAPHS (cont.)

	Time	Type of shot
Bride and groom eating cake		
During first dance (bride and groom)		
Bride and father dancing		
Groom and his mother dancing		
Musicians/DJ		
Leaving the reception		
Bride throwing her bouquet		
Good-byes		
Getting into the car		
Car leaving		
Special Requests		

Checklist 25 GUESTS' PHOTOGRAPH ORDERS					
Name	Address	Tel No	Proof No	Size	Qty

Video

Many brides now decide to have their wedding recorded on video, either in addition to or instead of photographs. The minister may not allow the service itself to be recorded on video but may permit some recording to take place.

As with photography, it is wise to check and compare the abilities and fees of professional firms.

An appointment with the videographer should be made as soon as possible after the wedding date is confirmed at which the schedule for the day should be discussed.

With the advancement of technological achievements and creative editing, professional videographers can now promise to produce tapes of exceptional quality.

Deciding on the right videographer involves research and as with many services, the best way to find a reliable one is through the recommendations of family or friends. The wedding photographer may be able to suggest a videographer with whom he has a good working relationship. It is only the professionals who have the appropriate equipment and skills to do the job correctly and it is worth taking the time and effort to find a reputable operator. He should use only broadcast quality cameras for the clearest and sharpest results. If a videographer shoots a wedding and then hands over the tape at the end of the day instead of doing the post-production work, then he has not done his job! When viewing samples of previous work, it is wise to look for smooth transitions, clear sound, proper lighting and sharp images.

Costs are based on the amount of editing done, the number and types of cameras used, the length of the wedding and special effects. Still photographs, names, titles and music all add polish to the final film, although too many effects can overdo the production making it look amateurish. Some packages include a one, one and a half or two hour finished tape; others are more condensed and easier to view, lasting for forty-five minutes. Few people, with the possible exception of the newly-weds, want to sit through a one hour tape. All the best moments can be captured in less than one hour. It is folly to feel that longer videos are the best value for money; the shorter video may be watched more frequently!

Attire

◆

Dress and Train

For a church wedding the bride may choose a full dress or something less formal. For second or late marriages her dress is often more restrained. There is no reason why a bride marrying in a register office cannot wear white if this is her choice.

Suppliers
Options for acquiring a dress include: specially made; ready-made from a specialist bridal wear shop or off-the-peg from a chain store or catalogue; second hand; hire; loan; self-made. Bridal dressmaking should be left to a professional unless the bride happens to be experienced.

Style
Magazines provide many ideas for style and should be perused before visiting the stores, otherwise the wealth of choice may prove bewildering! The key to successful outfitting seems to be the selection of a style that suits and coordination coupled with an awareness of the reality of shape and figure.

Head-dress
The veil is still the most popular bridal head-dress and must match the dress style. Alternatives include a small hat or cap, circlets of flowers, or ribbons trimmed with flowers.

Going-away Outfit
The going-away outfit can be anything the bride desires, but a wise choice would be something special that can be worn again afterwards.

Checklist 26 BRIDE'S ATTIRE

Wedding
   Dress supplier _____
   Address _____
   Tel _____
   Fitting dates _____
   Alteration dates _____
   Collection date _____
   Return date if hired _____
   Returner _____

		£
Dress		
Colour	_____	
Style	_____	
Measurements	_____	
Fabric	_____	
Trimmings	_____	
Head-dress	_____	
Footwear	_____	
Underwear	_____	
Accessories		
Gloves	_____	
Handbag	_____	
Jewellery	_____	
Something old	_____	
new	_____	
borrowed	_____	
blue	_____	
Make-up	_____	
Perfume	_____	
Payment details	_____	
Cancellation policy	_____	
Going-away outfit		
Outfit	_____	
Accessories	_____	
Payment details	_____	

Adult Male Members of the Wedding Party

The adult members of the wedding party, ie groom, best man, ushers and fathers of the bride and groom, should all dress alike. For most weddings, there are two main options, either morning dress (formal) or lounge suit (informal).

Traditional morning dress is usually a black or grey three-piece with a tail coat, or a black tail coat with pinstripe trousers. Accessories include a silk top hat, gloves and matching waistcoat. It is more usual to hire morning dress as it is very expensive to purchase.

Bridesmaids

The bridesmaids' dresses and accessories need to complement the bride's attire both in style and colour and should suit the girls themselves. There is no shortage of styles from which to choose.

Matron of Honour

A matron of honour would not wear a dress befitting a bridesmaid.

Flower Girl

A flower girl's role is usually purely decorative in that she will add some visual advantage to the attendants. Her outfit should be distinct from those of the bridesmaids.

Page Boys

Ideas for page boys' attire include: velvet jackets and grey trousers with bow tie; morning suit with top hat; Scottish outfit; sailor suit.

Mothers

The two mothers should consult the couple about style and colour scheme so that their outfits tone into an overall complementary scheme for the wedding party. Since they will be pictured together in the family group portraits and will both sit on the top table at the reception, they should ensure that they do not arrive at the church in the same outfit!

Guests

Guests can, of course, wear what they choose. Although the rule that all women in church wear hats has been relaxed in most parishes, because of the traditional nature of a wedding most will like to do so.

Hired Attire

For those members of the wedding party who intend to hire their outfits, it is important to start the search as early as possible so that there is ample time to make the right choice and allow the opportunity for several fittings. It is wise to obtain a written guarantee that the attire will be available on the wedding date and worth checking whether the attire will be available at some point prior to the wedding date so that an assessment can be made of the suitability of accessories and overall visual effect.

Compliance with collection and return dates is obviously of great importance. A list of wedding hire companies which are based all over the country is available on request with a stamped addressed envelope from *Brides Magazine*, Vogue House, Hanover Square, London W1R 0AD.

Checklist 27 ADULT MALES' ATTIRE		Groom	Best man	Bride's father
Name				
Supplier				
Address				
Tel				
Dates	Dress Rehearsal			
	Fittings			
	Alterations			
	Collection			
	Return			
	Returner			
Colour				
Style				
Sizes	Jacket			
	Trousers			
	Waistcoat			
	Shirt			
	Gloves			
	Top hat			
	Shoes			
	Socks			
Underwear				
Handkerchief				
Jewellery	Tie pin			
	Watch chain			
	Cufflinks			
Deposit				
Date due				
Balance				
Date due				
Going-away outfit			—	—
	£			

Groom's father	Ushers 1	Ushers 2	Ushers 3	Cost £
—	—	—	—	

Checklist 28 **ATTENDANTS' ATTIRE**	Chief bridesmaid	Bridesmaid 1	Bridesmaid 2
Name			
Dress supplier			
Address			
Tel			
Dates Fittings			
Alterations			
Collection			
Return			
Returner			
Dress Colour			
Style			
Measurements			
Fabric			
Trimmings			
Head-dress			
Footwear			
Underwear			
Accessories Gloves			
Handbag			
Jewellery			
Make-up			
Perfume			
Deposit			
Date due			
Balance			
Date due			
£			

Bridesmaid 3	Flower girl	Page boys	Matron of honour	COST £

Transport

◆ ◆ ◆

There are no strict rules concerning responsibility for transport except to emphasise that everyone must be transported safely.

Bride and her Family

The bride and her family are usually responsible for organising the following transport:

To church	Bride and giver-away Bride's mother, bridesmaids, flower girl and page boys
To reception	Bride and groom Attendants Parents of the bride and groom

Best Man

The best man is usually responsible for organising the following transport:

To church	Groom and best man
To reception	Best man, guests and ushers if necessary
From reception	Bride and groom

Checklist 29 **TRANSPORT**

Venues: Ceremony _____ Reception _____

	Supplier		Address		Tel	Notes
Booked						
Emergency						

	Organiser		Car booked	Chauf-feur booked	Times
	Bride ✔	Best man ✔			
To Church					
Bride and giver-away					
Bride's mother					
Bridesmaids					
Flower girl					
Page boys					
Groom's parents					
Ushers					
Groom and best man					
Guests					
£					

Checklist 29 **TRANSPORT** (cont.)					
	Organiser		Car booked	Chauf-feur booked	Times
	Bride ✔	Best man ✔			
To Reception					
Bride and groom					
Bridesmaids					
Flower girl					
Page boys					
Parents					
Ushers					
Best man					
Guests					
From Reception					
Bride and groom					
Bridesmaids					
Flower girl					
Page boys					
Parents					
Ushers					
Best man					
Guests					
£					

Rings and Gifts
for the
Wedding Party

❖ ◆ ❖

Rings

Although it is legal to be married without a ring, or to borrow a ring for the ceremony, it is more usual to have a new ring for the wedding. There is an extensive choice of rings from which to choose and it is worth shopping around prior to purchase.

Wedding rings are usually plain bands of yellow or white gold; they may be flat, rounded, carved or plain and should complement the engagement ring if they are to be worn together. Pure gold, which is 24 carats, is too soft for jewellery; 18 carat gold is serviceable and practical; 9 carat is harder, lighter in colour and more affordable.

Regarding fit, a ring which is slightly loose rather than tight will allow for growth of the fingers. If the ring is to be engraved, perhaps with the couple's initials or names and the wedding date, four to six weeks must be allowed.

Rings should be insured against loss, theft and damage for which the jeweller should provide a valuation certificate.

Gifts for the Couple,
the Wedding Party and Parents

The bride and groom sometimes exchange gifts to mark the special day. Gifts from the couple to their parents show appreciation for the wedding and gifts to the attendants express gratitude for their help. There is no reason for the gifts to be the same.

Checklist 30 **JEWELLERY & GIFTS**					
	Engagement		Wedding		
	Bride	Groom	Bride	Groom	Chief bridesmaid
Supplier					
Address					
Tel					
Gift					
Ring size					
Date rings ordered					
Details to be engraved					
Alterations					
Collection date					
Policy					
Exchange					
Return					
Refund					
Repair					
Replacement					
Guarantee					
Insurance					
Payment dates					
£					

Wedding					
Best man	Bridesmaids	Flower girl	Page boys	Ushers	Parents

Flowers

Wedding flowers complete and complement the bride's and bridesmaids' outfits and provide attractive displays both at church and the reception.

Bouquet

Bouquets are traditionally carried by the bride and bridesmaids. It is traditional for the bride to throw her bouquet backwards and over her shoulder towards the guests when she leaves for honeymoon. The one who catches it is supposed to be the next one to be married!

Alternatives to bouquets include: white prayer-book; Bible; parasol; fan; pomander; Dorothy bag with drawstrings.

Basket of Flowers

It is traditional for the flower girl to carry a basket of flowers.

Flower Arrangements

Flower arrangements for the church or register office and reception venue may complement the bride's and the bridesmaids' dresses.

Sprays

Sprays are for the mothers of the wedding couple.

Buttonholes

Buttonholes are usually for the principal men of the wedding party who normally wear white carnations.

Corsages

A corsage is a large buttonhole containing two or three large flowers. They are usually worn by the couple's mothers.

Checklist 31   FLOWERS

Florist

Address

Tel

	Colour	Style/shape	Flowers
BOUQUETS			
Bride			
Chief bridesmaid			
Bridesmaids			
BASKET			
Flower girl			
FLOWERS (Headdress)			
Bride			
Chief bridesmaid			
Bridesmaids			
Flower girl			
Page boys			
BUTTONHOLES			
Groom			
Best man			
Ushers			
Fathers			
CORSAGES			
Mothers			
FLOWER ARRANGEMENTS			
Church			
Altar			
Aisles (pew ends)			
Windows			
Reception			
Receiving line			
Tables: top, other, cake			
Cake			
£			

General flower style _____

General colour scheme _____

No.	Delivery	Collection	£	Payer

Parties

◆

Parties are a natural way of sharing with relatives and friends the happiness of a forthcoming or recent wedding.

Pre-wedding

Joint Families Social
Some couples host a party so that both sets of parents can meet, socialise and discuss wedding arrangements.

Rehearsal Get-together
It makes a pleasant event to have a small dinner party for the wedding party, and perhaps their partners, after the rehearsal at the church to show appreciation for the hard work that they will all be contributing to the special day. This is an ideal opportunity for the exchange of gifts.

Hen Night
The hen night is for the girls. Most brides like to hold their party a week or so before the wedding.

Stag Night
The stag night is for the boys and is usually organised by the best man. Transport arrangements need to be laid on and the best man must ensure that the groom returns home safely.

Post-wedding

It is traditional for the newly-weds to entertain both sets of parents, then the best man together with the bridesmaids and ushers sometime after the wedding at the couple's new home.

Gifts

Although it is traditional for guests to give presents, they have no obligation to do so, nor should the bride and her family feel that every donor should be 'rewarded' with an invitation to the wedding.

It is common practice today to circulate a gift list. Less expensive items should be included. Relatively expensive items may also be included since some people might like to club together to buy a single gift. Gifts for the home are still favourite.

Lists should be provided only upon request.

One master list may be sent with a letter of thanks and a request that it is ticked and passed on or returned. Alternatively, the list may be photocopied and distributed simultaneously, or it may be left at a local shop from where guests are advised to make their purchases.

Gifts should be addressed to the bride at her home and sent before the wedding so that the bride may despatch thank yous before the event.

The gifts may be displayed on the day for all to see, or displayed at the bride's home prior to the wedding.

Checklist 32 WEDDING GIFT LIST			
	Guests' choices	Colour	Model
Kitchen			
Dining room			
Lounge			
Hall, stairs and landing			
Master bedroom			
Spare bedroom			
Bathroom			
Garden, garage and DIY			
Home safety and security			
Personal items			
Miscellaneous			

Style	Design	Make	Size	Qty.	Available from

The Day

◆

Checklist 33	TIMETABLE	
TIME		NOTES
	Going-away attire and honeymoon provisions should be at the reception.	
-2 hrs	Bride makes up, dresses, prepares and transfers her engagement ring to her right hand.	
-40 mins	Ushers arrive at church, hand out order of service sheets ready to direct congregation to pews: bride's family and friends on the left and groom's on the right (facing the altar).	
-20 mins	The organ plays. Bell ringing commences. Guests arrive.	
-15 mins	Groom and best man arrive and pose for photographs. Best man pays fees to minister on behalf of groom. Best man checks on ushers. Groom and best man stand or sit in the front pew to the right of the aisle; the best man on the groom's right.	

Checklist 33	TIMETABLE (cont.)	
TIME		NOTES
-10 mins	Bridesmaids, flower girl, page boys and bride's mother gather in the church porch.	
-5 mins	Bride and giver-away arrive. Pose for photographs. Bride's mother adjusts bride's attire.	
-2 mins	Chief usher escorts bride's mother to her seat in the front pew on the left. Organist plays processional music. Ushers stand in back pews. Groom and best man rise and stand at the head of the aisle. Congregation stands. Bridesmaids and page boys form two columns and follow the bride and giver-away down the aisle. (The flower girl precedes the bride.) Procession proceeds with bride on giver-away's right arm. Meanwhile, groom and best man move from the front pew to the right of the chancel steps. At the chancel steps the bride is led by the giver-away to the groom's left. The chief bridesmaid lifts the bride's veil and takes her bouquet. Service commences and lasts for about 30 minutes. Vows and rings are exchanged. The couple are pronounced man and wife.	

Checklist 33	TIMETABLE (cont.)	
TIME		**NOTES**
	The service is concluded. The minister leads the bridal party into the vestry. The register is signed and witnessed. The bridal party leaves the church followed by the congregation from the front of the church. Chief usher checks the church to ensure that nothing has been left behind. Photographs are taken. The bride and groom leave for the reception followed by their parents and the attendants. At the reception, guests are received and welcomed. Guests are offered a drink. The best man signals the time for the meal to commence. The minister or best man says grace. Speeches and toasts commence. Cake-cutting ceremony. Cake slices are distributed. The bride and groom circulate and talk to guests and if possible this should be done while the couple are still in their wedding attire so that it may be admired by the guests at close range. At some point in the ensuing hours, the bride and groom change and leave for honeymoon after thanking the guests. It is polite for the couple	

Checklist 33	**TIMETABLE** (cont.)	
TIME		NOTES
	to thank privately those who have been particularly involved with the preparations. The host settles the reception account. The host, hostess and best man are last to leave.	

Afterwards

◆

Attire

Hired attire must be returned.

Press Report Following the Wedding

Details are contained under Announcements and Printing.

Cake

Small slices are sent by the bride's mother to those who were unable to attend on the day.

Thank-yous

Any outstanding notes of thanks need to be despatched.

Documentation

Name Change

Although it is traditional, and the most popular choice, for the bride to change her surname when she marries, there is no legal requirement for her to do so. She may retain her maiden name, in which case there is no need to change documents; she may use both names, for example using her maiden name for professional purposes and her married name socially; or she may unite the two names by joining them with a hyphen.

Unless the bride decides to keep her maiden name, it will be necessary to arrange for certain records to be amended. The following organisations should be informed in writing:

Checklist 34   DOCUMENTATION

	Date done
Employer	
Inland Revenue	
Department of Health	
Department of Social Security	
Electoral Roll	
Bank	
Credit card companies	
Building societies	
Post Office savings account	
Premium Bond office	
Insurance companies	
DVLC	
Passport office	
Doctor	
Dentist	
Clubs	
Associations	
Mail order catalogues	
Relatives	
Distant friends	
Others	

Index

◆

Figures in *italics* refer to checklists.

**Opening doors to
the World of books**

**Book Tokens
can be bought and
exchanged at most bookshops**